# First Book
# of Clarinet Solos

*Erstes Spielbuch für
Klarinette und Klavier*

edited and arranged by
JOHN DAVIES and PAUL READE

CLARINET IN B♭

KLARINETTE IN B

## Faber Music Limited
London

© 1983 by Faber Music Ltd
First published in 1983 by Faber Music Ltd
3 Queen Square London WC1N 3AU
Music drawn by Sheila Stanton
Cover design by Roslav Szaybo and Studio Gerrard
Printed in England

# Contents : Inhalt

Unless otherwise indicated, all arrangements are by Paul Reade.
*Alle Arrangements sind, wenn nicht anders angegeben, von Paul Reade.*

# Preface : Vorwort

The *First Book of Clarinet Solos* has been prepared for the true beginner on the instrument. The 28 pieces are arranged in an approximate order of difficulty to provide a wide range of music for study and performance. They should be practised and performed with careful attention to intonation, rhythm, dynamics, tone quality, character, style and deportment. The breath marks in the music should be observed, rounding off the phrases without over-shortening the final notes. The aim must be to match the flexibility and subtlety of the human voice. Tune your instrument carefully before playing and remember that the tuning may need to be adjusted later. Establish and maintain appropriate dynamic levels for the character and style of each piece.

The following forms of articulation are used:

♩ Tongued

♩ Staccato

♩ Tenuto

♩ ♩ Mezzo-staccato

♩ ♩ A lifted or shortened note – sustain the tonal level to the end of the lifted note

Das *Erste Spielbuch für Klarinette und Klavier* wurde für den reinen Anfänger auf dem Instrument zusammengestellt. Die 28 Stücke sind nach annähernd fortschreitendem Schwierigkeitsgrad angeordnet und umfassen ein großes Gebiet an musikalischer Literatur zum Üben und Aufführen. Die Stücke sollten unter genauer Beachtung von Intonation, Rhythmus, dynamischen Bezeichnungen, Klangqualität, Charakter und Stil der Musik und Haltung geübt und gespielt werden. Die Atemangaben sollten beachtet werden, da dadurch die Abrundung der Phrasen ohne allzu großes Verkürzen der letzten Noten erreicht wird. Es muß das Ziel sein, der Biegsamkeit und Subtilität der menschlichen Stimme gleichzukommen. Stimme das Instrument vor jedem Spielen sorgfältig und vergiß nicht, daß ein späteres Nachstimmen vonnöten sein kann. Spiele jedes Stück mit den seinem Charakter und Stil angemessenen Lautstärkegraden.

Folgende Artikulationsarten wurden verwendet:

♩ Angestoßen

♩ Stakkato

♩ Tenuto

♩ ♩ Mezzostakkato

♩ ♩ Die angebundene Note wird verkürzt, aber nicht angestoßen.

JOHN DAVIES
PAUL READE
Übersetzung: Dorothee Eberhardt

# I. PRELUDE

P.R.

# 2. SONG OF THE VOLGA BOATMEN

*Lied der Wolgaschiffer*

Traditional

# 3. PIERROT

Traditional

# 4.  RIDING ON A DONKEY

*Eselreiten*

Traditional

# 5. ROMANCE
## *Romanze*

P.R.

# 6. HATIKVAH

Hebrew Traditional

## 7. FINNISH FOLK SONG
*Finnisches Volkslied*

Traditional
arranged by Alan Richardson

8

# 8. SHEPHERD'S HEY

*Des Schäfers Hey*

Folk Dance

# 9. THE MERRY PEASANT

*Der fröhliche Landmann*

ROBERT SCHUMANN
(1810–1856)

# 10. SCHERZO

ANTON DIABELLI
(1781–1858)

## 11. THE APPLE FROM THE ORCHARD

*Der Apfel vom Obstgarten (El Pomo de lo Pomaro)*

Anon
(Venetian, c. 1520)

# 12. SERENADE: BEAUTIFUL DREAMER

*Serenade (Schöner Träumer)*

STEPHEN FOSTER
(1826-1864)

## 13. LÄNDLER

CARL REINECKE
(1824–1910)

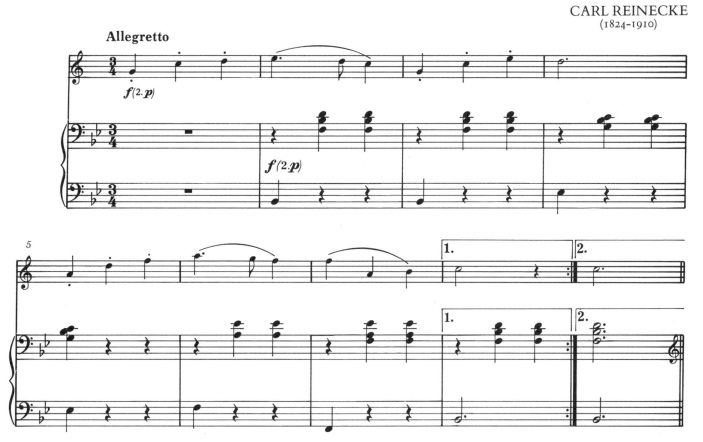

# 14. BERDOLIN'S SWEETHEART

*Berdolins Schatz (La cara cossa del Berdolin)*

Anon
(Venetian, c. 1520)

# 15. GERMAN DANCE

*Deutscher Tanz*

JOSEPH HAYDN
(1732–1809)

**TRIO**

*D.C. al Fine*

# 16. BY THE FIRESIDE
## *Am Kamin*

ROBERT SCHUMANN
(1810–1856)

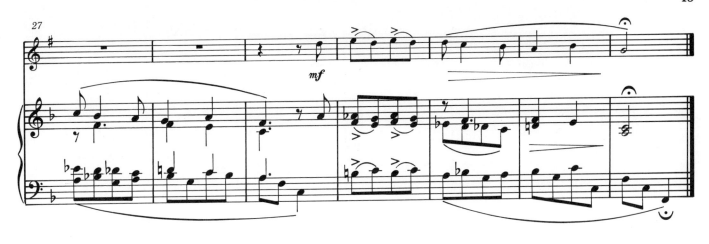

## 17. REVERIE
*Träumerei*

PYOTR TCHAIKOVSKY
(1840-1893)

## 18. LULLABY
*Wiegenlied*

WOLFGANG AMADEUS MOZART
(1756-1791)
arranged by Alan Richardson

# 19. RONDEAU

HENRY PURCELL
(1659–1695)
arranged by Alan Richardson

# 20. TO A WILD ROSE

*An eine wilde Rose*

EDWARD MACDOWELL
(1861-1908)

26

## 21. CONTREDANSE
*Kontertanz*

JEAN-PHILIPPE RAMEAU
(1683-1754)

(original)

Fine

*p*

D. C. al Fine

## 22. ANDANTE

JOHANNES BRAHMS
(1833-1897)

Andante (♩=66)

*p espressivo, semplice*

*p semplice*

*più*

28

## 23. MINUET
*Menuett*

JOHANN SEBASTIAN BACH
(1685-1750)

## 24. TRIO

WOLFGANG AMADEUS MOZART
(1756-1791)

# 25. THE FASCINATOR
## *Der Bezauberer*

JAMES SCOTT
arranged by David Matthews

## 26. ★ ★ ★

ROBERT SCHUMANN
(1810-1856)
arranged by Alan Richardson

# 27. WHEN DAISIES PIED

*Wenn Primeln gelb*

THOMAS ARNE
(1710-1778)

# 28. THEME
## *Thema*

FRANZ SCHUBERT
(1797-1828)

1. Well-marked rhythm and precise articulation will help this piece to sound like a dance. Observe the dynamics carefully.

2. A Russian work-song, requiring firm and sonorous tone with gentle articulation. Notes marked ♩ are sustained, with a slight stress.

3. This piece is lighthearted in character. Observe the difference between ♩ ♩. and ♩ (with accent)

4. In this lively tune differentiate between detached and staccato notes.

5. Gentle and reflective playing is required. Throat notes (g′ and a′) need extra breath support. Notes of the same pitch beneath a slur are lightly articulated.

6. A Hebrew anthem, to be played with a rich, cantabile tone.
   The acciaccatura in bar 16 must not deprive the principal note of its natural accent.

7. A peasant song, wistful in character, with some opportunity for rubato.

8. 'I will play on the tabor to the worthies, and let them dance the Hey' (Shakespeare: *Love's Labours Lost*). This country dance should be played with vigour. Count four in a bar in bars 10–12 and 14–16 until they are secure.

9. From Schumann's *Album for the Young*. Maintain the evenness of tone, indicating the shape and direction of each phrase.

10. Vivacious music, needing accents on the first beat of each bar. A lifted note marked ♩ (with tenuto/staccato) is not tongued but shortened.

11. A lively dance needing a firm, swinging rhythm, with 2 beats in a bar.

12. A famous song by Stephen Foster evoking the spirit of the American deep south.

13. A German country dance in triple time. The second and third beats of each bar should be lightened.

14. Imagine the raucous sound of the shawm in this robust piece. Pay particular attention to the piano part in the final three bars to ensure accuracy of ensemble.

15. From Haydn's set of *12 German Dances* (1792). It is in ternary form with a central Trio contrasting with the repeated first section.

16. From Schumann's piano pieces *Scenes from Childhood*. Be aware of the dynamic level and the natural direction of the phrases. Take care over the entry in bar 12.

17. This *Reverie* (day-dream) is from Tchaikovsky's *Children's Pieces*. The figure ♩. ♪ needs to be rhythmically exact, and played with precise finger movements.

18. A tender, expressive song by Mozart. Use mezzo-staccato articulation with two gentle stresses per bar.

19. From the incidental music to Shakespeare's *A Midsummer Night's Dream*.

20. An arrangement of a well-known piece from the American composer Edward MacDowell's *Woodland Sketches*. It needs a warm, romantic tone.

21. A vivacious country dance. Accent the first beat of each bar to give movement and vitality, and use a light staccato articulation.

22. The theme from the slow movement of Brahms' 3rd Symphony. Lyrical, sustained playing is required with lightly articulated semiquavers.

23. This graceful minuet is one of a number of keyboard pieces written by Bach for his wife Anna Magdalena. Each of the four-bar phrases should be played in one breath.

24. This clarinet melody, from the Minuet and Trio of Mozart's Symphony no. 39, requires broad phrasing. In the symphony the staccato quavers in the accompaniment are played by the second clarinet.

25. James Scott was a popular American composer of piano ragtime music. The syncopated, tied notes should have a slight accent.

26. This untitled piece from Schumann's *Album for the Young* should be played cantabile with great expressiveness. The turn ∾ in the penultimate bar should be played

27. A lyrical setting of the song *When daisies pied and violets blue* sung by Spring, in Shakespeare's *Love's Labour's Lost*. Observe the varying articulation marks.

28. The theme, originally for clarinet in C, from the Theme and Variations of Schubert's Octet. The theme was taken by Schubert from his own early opera *Die Freunde von Salamanka*. The dotted rhythm, grace notes and staccato articulations must not interrupt the flow of the melody. The trill in the penultimate bar may be played

1. Ein markant betonter Rhythmus und genaue Artikulation werden dazu beitragen, dieses Stück wie einen Tanz klingen zu lassen. Achte sorgfältig auf die dynamischen Bezeichnungen.

2. Ein russischen Arbeitslied, das einen kräftigen, vollen Ton und sanfte Artikulation verlangt. Mit ♩ bezeichnete Noten werden ausgehalten und leicht akzentuiert.

3. Dieses Stück ist fröhlichen, sogar humorvollen Charakters. Beachte den Unterschied zwischen ♩ ♩ und ♩ .

4. Unterscheide in diesem lebhaften Stück zwischen voneinander getrennten und mit Stakkato bezeichneten Noten.

5. Dieses Stück verlangt sanftes, nachdenkliches Spiel. Die Töne g′ und a′ brauchen besondere Atemunterstützung. Zwei Noten der gleichen Tonhöhe unter einem Bogen werden leicht angestoßen.

6. Eine hebräische Hymne, die mit einem runden, ausdrucksvollen Ton zu spielen ist. Der Vorschlag in Takt 16 darf die nachfolgende Hauptnote nicht ihres natürlichen Akzents berauben.

7. Ein Bauernlied von wehmütigem Charakter, das einige Male Gelegenheit zu Rubato gibt.

8. 'Ich will den Würdigen mit dem Tamburin aufspielen und sie den Hey tanzen lassen' (Shakespeare: *Verlorene Liebesmüh*). Dieser Volkstanz sollte mit Energie und Ausdruck gespielt werden. Zähle Viertel in den Takten 10-12 und 14-16 bis diese geläufig sind.

9. Aus Schumanns *Album für die Jugend*. Behalte die Gleichmäßigkeit des Tones bei, die für Form und Verlauf einer jeden Phrase wichtig ist.

10. Eine lebhafte Musik, bei der der jeweils erste Taktschlag betont werden muß. Eine mit ♩ bezeichnete Note wird nicht angestoßen, sondern verkürzt.

11. Ein lebendiger Tanz, der einen gleichmäßig eingehaltenen, swingenden Rhythmus mit zwei Taktschlägen pro Takt erfordert.

12. Ein berühmtes Lied von Stephen Foster, das den Geist des tiefen Südens Amerikas beschwört.

13. Ein deutscher Volkstanz im Dreiertakt. Die jeweils zweiten und dritten Taktschläge sollten kaum betont werden.

14. Denke bei diesem frischen, urwüchsigen Stück an den rauhen Klang der Schalmei. Achte besonders auf die drei letzten Takte der Klavierbegleitung um genaues Zusammenspiel zu gewähren.

15. Aus den *12 Deutschen Tänzen* (1792) von Haydn. In dreiteiliger Form, wobei das Trio in der Mitte mit dem wiederholten ersten Teil kontrastiert.

16. Aus Schumanns Klavierstücken *Kinderszenen*. Denke an die Lautstärke und den natürlichen Verlauf der Phrasen. Achte besonders auf den Einsatz in Takt 12.

17. Diese *Reverie*, 'Träumerei' stammt aus Tschaikovskys *Kinderstücken*. Die Figur ♪.♪ muß rhythmisch exakt gespielt werden; die Koordination der Fingerbewegungen ist besonders wichtig.

18. Ein zartes, ausdrucksvolles Lied von Mozart. Spiele mit mezzostakkato Artikulation und betone beide Takthälften leicht.

19. Aus der Bühnenmusik zu Shakespeares *Ein Mittsommernachtstraum*.

20. Ein Arrangement eines bekannten Stückes aus den *Woodland Sketches* des amerikanischen Komponisten Edward MacDowell. Es erfordert einen warmen, romantischen Ton.

21. Ein lebhafter Volkstanz. Betone den jeweils ersten Taktschlag um Bewegung und Vitalität zu erreichen, und spiele mit leichtem Stakkatoanstoß.

22. Das Thema des langsamen Satzes aus der dritten Symphonie von Brahms. Es verlangt lyrisches, verhaltenes Spiel mit leicht artikulierten Sechzehnteln.

23. Dieses anmutige Menuett gehört zu einer Anzahl von Stücken für Tasteninstrument, die Bach für seine Frau Anna Magdalena geschrieben hat. Jede der viertaktigen Phrasen sollte mit einem Atem gespielt werden.

24. Diese Klarinettenmelodie aus dem 'Menuett und Trio' von Mozarts Symphonie Nr. 39 erfordert eine weitgespannte Phrasierung. In der Symphonie werden die Stakkatoachtel der Begleitung von der zweiten Klarinette gespielt.

25. James Scott war ein populärer amerikanischer Komponist von Ragtimemusik für Klavier. Die synkopierten, gebundenen Noten sollten leicht akzentuiert werden.

26. Dieses unbetitelte Stück aus Schumanns *Album für die Jugend* sollte cantabile und mit viel Ausdruck gespielt werden. Der Doppelschlag ∞ im vorletzten Takt sollte so gespielt werden:

27. Eine lyrische Vertonung des Liedes *Wenn Primeln gelb und Veilchen blau*, gesungen vom Frühling in Shakespeares *Verlorene Liebesmüh*. Beachte die verschiedenartigen Artikulationsangaben.

28. Das Thema von 'Thema und Variationen' aus Schuberts Oktett, ursprünglich für C-Klarinette. Schubert entnahm es seiner eigenen frühen Oper *Die Freunde von Salamanka*. Der punktierte Rhythmus, die Verzierungen und die Stakkatoartikulation dürfen den Melodiefluß nicht hemmen. Der Triller im vorletzten Takt kann so gespielt werden:

Printed by Halstan & Co. Ltd., Amersham, Bucks., England